So Christ himself gave the apostles, the prophets, the evangelists, the pastors and teachers, to equip his people for works of service, so that the body of Christ may be built up until we all reach unity in the faith and in the knowledge of the Son of God and become mature, attaining to the whole measure of the fullness of Christ.

Ephesians 4:11-13

MULTI-SITE MINISTRY

Expanding the Expedition Reach

Ken Nash

with Kristen Farrell

the greatest
EXPEDITION

MULTI-SITE MINISTRY

Expanding the Expedition Reach

©2021 Ken Nash

books@marketsquarebooks.com
P.O. Box 23664 Knoxville, Tennessee 37933
ISBN: 978-1-950899-27-2

Printed and Bound in the United States of America
Cover Illustration & Book Design ©2021 Market Square Publishing, LLC
Publisher: Kevin Slimp
Editors: Kristin Lighter & Kay Kotan

This resource was commissioned as
one of many interconnected steps in the
journey of *The Greatest Expedition*.

GreatestExpedition.com

Table of Contents

Foreword

This resource was commissioned as one of many interconnected steps in the journey of *The Greatest Expedition*. While each step is important individually, we intentionally built the multi-step Essentials Pack and the Expansion Pack to provide a richer and fuller experience with the greatest potential for transformation and introducing more people to a relationship with Jesus Christ. For more information, visit GreatestExpedition.org.

However, we also recognize you may be exploring this resource apart from *The Greatest Expedition*. You might find yourself on a personal journey, a small group journey, or perhaps a church leadership team journey.

We are so glad you are on this journey!

As you take each step in your expedition, your Expedition Team will discover whether the ministry tools you will be exploring will be utilized only for the Expedition Team or if this expedition will be a congregational journey. Our hope and prayer is *The Greatest Expedition* is indeed a congregational journey, but if it proves to be a solo journey for just the Expedition Team, God will still do amazing things through your intentional exploration, discernment, and faithful next steps.

Regardless of how you came to discover *The Greatest Expedition,* it will pave the way to a new God-inspired expedition. Be brave and courageous on your journey through *The Greatest Expedition!*

Kay L Kotan, PCC
Director, *The Greatest Expedition*

CHAPTER ONE
Why Should We Multi-site?

Many churches come to a point in their journey where they have to answer questions regarding growth and expansion. This often leads to tiresome building campaigns, heated discussion about missional versus attractional models of ministry, and the like. However, a closer look at the multi-site movement will help answer many of the questions you may have. A multi-site ministry is one church meeting in several locations while sharing a common vision, budget, resources, leadership structure and strategy. Most importantly, the multi-site movement reminds us that we are truly better together and reaches a new generation of church-goers who desire to worship in their home communities. Its exponential growth in recent years reflects today's attempt to offer effective ministry in places our local ministries previously lacked the ability to reach. There are several reasons to consider an expedition into multi-site ministry, but here we are going to explore the primary reasons why multi-site is both biblical and preferable.

It aligns with God's consistent call to multiply.

Have you ever considered the first command in Scripture? Adam and Eve were told to be fruitful and multiply.[1] They were to take dominion over the land, which, in essence, was a call to go. Abraham and Moses were to do likewise. Isaiah later proclaimed, "the Lord has sent me to bring good news to the oppressed."[2] This later became the clear mission of Jesus who modeled the practice of multiplication and sending throughout his ministry. While training his disciples, Jesus called them to "be" with him and then, after

---

[1] Genesis 1:28

[2] Isaiah 61:1

being trained, "to be sent out"[3] to do kingdom building work. This led to Jesus' Great Commission to the church. From its inception, the call to "go and make disciples" has been the mandate for the church throughout the world. As churches were planted throughout the land, Paul led a network of worshiping communities that were unified under common practices, mission and beliefs, but not necessarily under one roof in one building.

Years later, as the Protestant Reformation took shape; the Methodist circuit riders offered another excellent precedent for this type of ministry as they traveled on horseback to preach at multiple churches. Francis Asbury, the founding bishop of American Methodism, traveled more than a quarter of a million miles on foot and horseback, preaching about sixteen thousand sermons as he worked his circuits.[4]

Today, Craig Groeschel, Lead Pastor of

---

[3] Mark 3:14

[4] Driscoll, Mark, and Gerry Breshears. *Vintage Church: Timeless Truths and Timely Methods.* Wheaton: Crossway, 2009. Pg 245.

a large multi-site ministry, believes this move from horseback to satellite broadcast is simply a shift from the circuit rider of the past to a closed-circuit rider of the present.[5] The multi-site movement keeps the church centered on God's consistent call to go and make disciples for the transformation of the world while staying connected to one another in community.

It gives a greater ability to contextualize.

Multi-site allows a ministry to enhance its local impact while expanding its demographic reach into unique spaces and places. Urban ministry is certainly different from rural or suburban ministries. Additionally, with the ever-widening cultural and social gaps developing throughout society, the need for the church to adapt as an institution and unify those around us has never been greater. Simply put, launching a new campus offers your church the best opportunity to overcome

---

[5] Surratt, Geoff, Greg Ligon, and Warren Bird. *The Multi-Site Church Revolution: Being One Church in Many Locations.* Grand Rapids: Zondervan, 2006. Pg 91.

many geographic and/or cultural barriers present as you move into new communities. We are a diverse nation, and sadly, Sunday morning is known to be the most segregated day of the week. In order to meet individual communities' needs, the church needs to stay relevant regardless of age, race, gender, socio-economic status, education, or culture. The Gospel message truly is for everyone, and a one size fits all approach is dated and culturally tone deaf. Galatians 3:28 reminds us that, "There is neither Jew nor Gentile, neither slave nor free, nor is there male and female, for you are all one in Christ Jesus." Multi-site allows for individual personality while maintaining a church's DNA.

Moreover, as the church was literally forced to leave the building during the COVID-19 pandemic, many people established new patterns of faith expression. For many, it was no longer necessary to gather in person as their on-line community and personal practices satisfied many of their spiritual needs. Multi-site allows for the church to be more agile when responding to unprecedented times and situations, offering specialized support to reach new people and to keep faithful congregants engaged.

It engages far more people in the ministry.

Because each additional site requires an entirely new team, the laity are essential for success. Through a study of one thousand multi-site churches, Warren Bird and Kristin Walters found that four out of five churches reported an increase in lay engagement. Dave Ferguson confirmed this as new campuses grew at Christian Community Church: "We were forced to develop 100 spiritual entrepreneurs who would see this as a missional opportunity. It gave people the motivation and opportunity to grow as never before."[6]

Additionally, as people become more engaged, there is more buy in for the greater mission of both the new site, as well as for the sending site. Conversely, as large

---

[6] Bird, Warren, and Kristin Walters. "Multisite Is Multiplying: New Development in the Movement's Expansion." *Leadnet.* Leadership Network, 2 Sept. 2010. Web. 31 Dec. 2011. Pg 13.

churches expand, a general malaise can set in as congregants fail to see the gaps in ministry as many appear already to be filled. A sense of not being needed is an unwanted culture to create, knowing that God has gifted each follower of Christ a specific purpose to be lived out as a part of the whole body. Regardless of church size, to be a growing and thriving congregation, people need to be engaged in serving, but with the multi-site model, one person's willingness to serve is more evident and arguably more contagious.

It lightens everyone's load through shared resources.

We are better together. When launching a new campus, this becomes evident in the following ways:

Shared leadership: In traditional church plants, the sending congregation often loses high-capacity leaders to the new plant, leaving a felt void. Multi-site ministry allows all locations to continue to benefit from the various leaders throughout the entire church, regardless of which campus they attend.

Shared workload: From message planning and leadership training, to budget production and curriculum production, many hands make light work. Therefore, the pastor who oversees the location can focus on evangelism, shepherding and making disciples rather than spending time in weekly message preparation, planning and writing or attending meetings. This is the same for various departments whether it is the worship team, youth ministry, or early childhood. As directors work together, they experience less burn out as one ministry area has many high level participants involved.

Shared support: The commitment of an established congregation in prayer, resources and relationships provides a solid base that is not as available to a smaller, independent church plant. This can be as simple as a high-output copy machine or as complex as a faithful prayer team who has shown up dutifully for years of early morning prayer. A small struggling congregation doesn't have to worry about managing so many administrative details that could possibly hinder ministry when there is shared support from the sending campus. Something as seemingly un-spiritual as a roof leak can be taken care of with relative ease instead of the possibility of it stopping services for a weekend when there is support, and hopefully a contractor, across campuses!

Shared reputation: As the new site launches in a neighboring location, it carries with it the name of the larger church network. That healthy brand reputation often gives guests some confidence in checking out the site near them. This awareness gives multi-sites credibility that may take years to establish when entering a new community. Conversely, there is an unwritten accountability from the established church to not work for the approval of people, but to definitely be aware of the reputation that it has earned in its community. In these instances, iron does indeed sharpen iron.

Multi-site ministry is worthy of consideration as a part of any healthy church's strategy moving forward. Of the thousands of multi-site ministries surveyed in Leadership Network's research, 82 percent reported annual attendance growth.[7] As a leader, I often do a cost-benefit analysis before making a final decision. In the case of multi-site, the benefits far outweigh the cost.

It enjoys the benefits of small churches while growing larger.

Large churches offer more opportunities and variation in ministry than smaller congregations, including a wider support system and network. At the same time, worshiping communities of several hundred (rather than several thousand) are frequently more relational and intimate, offering a more connected and accountable environment which often promotes greater spiritual growth. The evidence clearly reveals that multiple sites reach more people. With more people comes a wider variety of fresh ministry expressions, yet the intimacy and connection remains higher in smaller worshiping venues.

---

[7] Ligon, Greg, Whitehead, Josh, Travis, Dave, Mavity, Chris. "Multisite Movement Continues to Grow" https://leadnet.org/multisite-movement-survey-2019.

There is much talk today about millennials and the generations who will follow. Some good talk and others, not so much. However, a few things are evident by taking a quick look at popular culture movements. Shop local. Support small business. Be authentic. Giving Tuesday. Locally grown. Get involved. Farm to table. What all of these ideas have in common, the multi-site model supports. These ideas are the bread and butter of what millennials are buying into these days – and with vigor and purpose. Generations to follow are embracing more vulnerability and less perfection, more doing and less watching, and smaller communities in place of mega churches. Relationships are at the core of the human experience, and despite the fact that many positive and compelling relationships are found in large congregations, the preference is to find these deep and impactful relationships in smaller communities where their voices can be heard. Additionally, as these multi-sites are woven together with a greater purpose and mission, a sense of the greater good, the unending and persistent desire to share the Gospel to build the kingdom, is evident in growing numbers.

CHAPTER TWO

The Common Types of Multi-Site

The Video-Venue Model

In this model, the sending church site casts sermons, live or previously recorded, to the other sites. It typically offers live worship music and a campus pastor to give a consistent voice and a point person as the campus pastor delivers announcements, pastoral care, and on-site leadership.

Advantages:

- Gathering space is flexible

- DNA of the sending church is easily replicated with video messages

- Communication between the campuses remains very clear

Disadvantages:

- Campus is dependent on primary communicator

- Campus often becomes an independent church after the main communicator leaves

- Technology expenses are often high because of needed ongoing upgrades

The Teaching Team Model

In this live preaching approach, the lead pastor typically writes the sermons in collaboration with the campus pastors and other teaching team members. Each teaching pastor preaches the same material at each of the campuses but has the freedom to illustrate in innovative ways or to highlight an established idea in a more pronounced way. Each pastor preaches on the same scriptures, emphasizes the same central ideas but may choose varied stylistic approaches to personalize the material in order to own the message in a connected way.

Advantages:

- New preachers are trained up for the teaching ministry

- Increased creativity in messages as more preachers contribute ideas

- Prayer support and accountability is felt among the teaching team

- Provides continued feedback and sharpening of one another's gifts

- Fresh voices in the pulpit offer varied strengths and perspectives for congregants

- Avoids a personality driven church

- Helps decrease pulpit burnout for lead pastors

Disadvantages:

- Difficult to replicate similar worship atmosphere in various campuses due to personality differences, thus they may create their own DNA

- Increased potential for comparison and competition

- Vision may weaken between campuses as a result of varied perspectives

- Congregants feel less connected to multiple voices

The Merger or Adoption Models

These models have become increasingly more common as long time existing churches age and begin facing financial and/or attendance crises. As of 2019, 40 percent of all multi-sites begin as a merger where a dying church is absorbed by a healthier local church[8]. These models allow the current ministry to sit dormant within the community for an extended time (preferably three to six months), allowing the community to notice the lack of activity.

As one planter stated, "We let the grass grow in the parking lot." Therefore, when the new ministry restarts under the new name, there is a stark difference in community engagement, landscaping, signage and branding as the ministry comes back to life in tangible ways.

Advantages:

- Continued faith-based presence in the community

---

[8] https://www.aspengroup.com/blog/four-questions-to-ask-if-youre-considering-a-church-merger.

- Increased popularity as many dying churches relinquish old patterns

- Breathes life into a stale, but solid foundation and community presence

Disadvantages:

- Continued residual issues of former church DNA

- Carry-over of the old and possibly poor reputation in the community

- Outdated facilities may be costly to update

- Only partial relinquished past, causing division of vision

The Missional Campus Model

A missional campus has the most flexibility and fluidity. The Missional Campus Model sends groups from the church to start small communities of faith in atypical locations. This model begins with a heart of serving, meeting the basic needs of the community around them. This often starts organically through natural relationships such as establishing various forms of co-ops that meet basic needs around food or clothing through donations and grants.

Advantages:

- Rapid start up with low financial commitment

- Easy to multiply

- Reaches a new demographic

Disadvantages:

- Harder to gain critical mass

- Existing church may have difficulty seeing it as a legitimate campus

- Limited exposure to the gifts and personalities of others in the church

Community Partnership Model

This model produces meaningful relationships with local business leaders and community influencers while collaborating with the local YMCA, bar, restaurant, community center, prison, hospital, etc. in which the campus is located. This happens as space and resources are used to mutually benefit one another.

Advantages:

- Builds relationship within the community

- Reaches a new mission field with minimal risk

Disadvantages:

- Competition for space

- Dependent on the sustainability and reliability of the owner. If the local business fails, the ministry needs to rapidly find a new location or rebuild a relationship with the new business owner.

- Outsiders attaching the church mission to the connected business/venue's mission and values

Online Virtual Campus *Priority or? Distraction.*

Nearly all of the churches in America became multi-site during the Covid-19 Pandemic because of the need for a virtual campus and an online presence. As churches were initially forced to worship online, they were given a unique opportunity to experience, expand, and, hopefully, refine this form of ministry. Because of this, many churches are now hiring online pastors to connect with a demographic of people who would likely never attend church in person or a demographic of people who are unable to attend.

Advantages:

- Reaches a new generation in relevant ways, meeting them "where they're at"

- Cost effective because there isn't facility maintenance other than technical equipment

- Allows for new attendees to "visit" in a comfortable setting

- Can multiply rapidly and feed into an in-person campus

Disadvantages:

- Misses the beauty of a worshiping community by limiting experiences with the full body of Christ, thus reducing meaningful connections

- Limited exposure to the gifts and personalities of others in the church

- Reduces opportunities to serve in various areas of giftedness

- Can easily lose the identity and vision of the sending church

CHAPTER THREE
Multiplication Readiness
Self-Assessment

While multi-site ministry has a high success rate, the new campus's vitality is not guaranteed. Therefore, it is wise for the leadership to take inventory of the health of their entire ministry prior to embarking on this expedition. New campuses have a way of exposing the unhealthy parts of the current ministry. Therefore, it is imperative that evaluation happens before the new campus is launched. While I highly recommend deeper evaluative tools such as *Readiness 360*,[9] the following is a checklist that will help you begin the process of evaluating the health of your ministry through open conversation with the existing leadership team. Reflecting on and assessing the

---

[9] https://readiness360.org/

evidence of the following eight ideas will ensure a strong probability of success in launching and sustaining other campuses.

Evidence of God's timing

When a church is naturally ready to reproduce, God stirs the hearts of the people. There is a natural rush of excitement that builds throughout the ministry. The energy is tangible as the chatter of expectancy heightens. People show up for informational meetings with questions and curiosity. The anticipation and commitment level builds with very little manufactured energy from the church leadership. In short, the evidence of God's timing for the launch is obvious.

We experienced this in our last site launch. Our church was asked to adopt a parachurch ministry a few years ago. It was a nonprofit ministry similar to a Goodwill, combining drop off donations and a thrift store as well as a food pantry. At the time, we did not have a worshiping presence in that community but did have many families who lived in that city who drove 20 miles to attend our church for weekend services. As God opened doors for this ministry, we called those families together for a meeting to see if there was any interest in this ministry. Thirty people showed up to this initial meeting. Ten people agreed to get involved. One person wanted to become the director over the entire organization. The energy was palpable. As we gained traction in that community by building relationships, we started a partnership with another local church who asked if we would consider adopting them as described previously in the adoption model. Over the next year, we saw evidence of God's provision and guidance as we asked questions about coming together as one. While it was not effortless and was not immediate (this was a three-year process!), there was evidence of God's timing throughout the entire journey.

We have all been in situations where we push our own agenda instead of being open to God's perfect plan. First and foremost, God must be the head of the church as we explore different models of reaching people with the Gospel message. God often works through circumstances and opportunities.

These opportunities need to be prayed over with discernment from elders and lay people alike. Multi-site requires a team, not just an individual. And it is obvious that with any prompting of God, you will see tangible moments of clarity toward a potential launch of a campus.

Theological and Missional Alignment

Never underestimate the power of unified focus. Light in a room is certainly beneficial, but when that light is focused and pointed in the same direction it becomes a laser, able to cut through the hardest of surfaces. If leadership is currently divided over theological issues or a missional purpose, it would be wise to come to a focused agreement first. Multi-site can rapidly splinter ministry overall if its core convictions and purposes are not in alignment.

I was working with a church several years ago that inspired this check point. Their leadership was divided, and they knew it. However, their desire to be a multi-site ministry was stronger than the tension they felt with one another. The campus pastor, along with several leaders on the launch team, wanted the campus to value a fully inclusive ministry regarding sexuality and the LGBTQ+ community. The sending church did not see that as a primary value. To complicate matters, the division was not initially discovered. Some of these differing convictions are, quite frankly, the hardest pitfall to detect. I am not concerned about the person who loudly disputes the church's vision. That is very easy to identify, address, and reach consensus on. My greatest concern is the leader or pastor who is only one degree off from our theological and missional values. While that may not seem significant, it is. Consider this, being one degree off on a compass will land you miles off course the further along on your journey. Do you and your team a favor, have some deeper conversations about your theology and your mission prior to the development of your launch strategy. This will naturally feed the next checkpoint.

Clearly Articulated Vision.

Multisite is NOT the *vision* of the church. Multisite is the tool your church will use to implement the church's vision. So let me ask you, is your vision clear? Is it worthy of reproduction through the launch of a new ministry location? Your vision should answer questions such as, where are we headed or what are we aiming for as a ministry. Your vision should look toward the future of what your ministry hopes to achieve.

Vision statements are typically memorable, concise and inspirational. Dave Ferguson, pastor of Christian Community Church in the greater Chicago area, said, "if your church's vision cannot be easily written on a napkin it is likely not going to be remembered." If it can be drawn or written out on a napkin, your average attender can describe the church's vision to their friend during a quick lunch date. Here are some examples.

- Christian Community Church Vision: To help people find their way back to God.

- Watermark Wesleyan Church Vision: To discover wholeness in Jesus.

- Church of the Resurrection Vision: To be used by God to change lives, strengthen churches, and transform the world.

When your church is launching a new campus, it is imperative that as many of your regular attendees are able to describe the ministry to the community. They become the greatest catalyst for growing the church and knowing the vision will invest individuals into its greater purpose. For some, this may be the first step taken to initiate a healthy and effective launch.

Small groups —> ?
? ? ?

Effective Disciple-Making Pipeline

One of the criticisms of launching campuses often comes from those left behind at the sending location(s). New sites frequently draw high-energy people who have a pioneering spirit. When a church sends a large number of passionate people to the new campus, it can leave a sizable void behind both in function and energy. For a church to counteract that, it takes intentional training. The Apostle Paul clearly articulated this to his protégé, Timothy. *"Timothy, what you have heard from me through many witnesses entrust to faithful people who will be able to teach others as well"* (2 Timothy 2: 2). Churches that are effective in reproducing disciples in a similar manner find great success in ministry.

God used this disciple-making pipeline to advance the movement of the Wesleyan revival of the 1700s. *Warning:* What you are about to read may not be suitable for some ego-driven preachers. John Wesley wrote,

> *I was more convinced than ever that the preaching like an Apostle without joining together those that are awakened and training them up in the ways of God is only begetting children for the murderer. How much preaching there has been for these 20 years all over Pembrookeshire. But no regular societies, no discipline, no order or connection, and the consequence is that 9 in 10 of the once awakened are now faster asleep than ever...One hour in a band (small group) is more effective than 10 years of preaching.*[10]

In other words, when we solely rely on preaching from the pulpit to impact lives in a transformative way, we will always come up short. Far too many churches today have congregations that are "now faster asleep than ever." Without discipleship, people are free to take from the church an inspiring lesson without accountability or action. When

---

[10] John Wesley, *Wesley's Works, Vol. III,* Grand Rapids: Baker Book House, 1979, pg 144.

people are intentionally connected for prayer, study and spiritual development, a contagious spiritual growth naturally and effectively occurs. Do you have an intentional plan for discipling people within your church?

Lay Empowerment is the Norm.

[handwritten: All Leaders should be called Pastor]

Penn State sociologists Roger Finke and Rodney Stark report that the early Methodists clearly embraced the priesthood of all believers by starting up churches with lay leadership. When the circuit rider was not available during the week, the local church had a class leader (lay person) who pastored until the circuit rider could return. Using that approach, Methodists became one of the largest religious groups in the United States, moving from "less than 2.5 percent of church adherents in 1776 to more than 34.2 percent in 1850," which was a growth from sixty-five congregations to 13,302 in just seventy years. The reason for this growth was described as "local amateur lay pastors" who fulfilled the duties of the pastor in lieu of the absent circuit riders. However, it wasn't sustained. Finke and Stark's final analysis of that time in history reveals the following:

[handwritten: # emails "Appreciate the Pastor month"????]

The dramatic metric rise of the Methodists was short-lived. It is instructive to note that the Methodists began to slump at precisely the same time that their amateur clergy were replaced by professionals who claimed episcopal authority over their congregations.[11]

Of course, we need the "professionals" to develop, grow, and lead our ministries, however, in all of my years of coaching churches, I have never heard a church say we have enough hired staff. Even the healthiest of churches always claim to be one or two staff persons short of feeling like they have "arrived." Church leader, hear this – you will never have enough paid staff to accomplish all you are hoping to accomplish in ministry. Stop chasing that carrot. Instead, start empowering laity. When laity get empowered, the ministry has the opportunity to blossom in previously unforeseen ways. Therefore, it is quite easy to predict a successful launch when leading by laity is already the culture

---

[11] Finke, Roger, and Rodney Stark. "How the Upstart Sects Won America: 1776-1850." *Journal for the Scientific Study of Religion* 28.1 (1989): 27. Academic Search Premier. Dec. 2011.

of the church thus empowering even more congregants to move forward in ministry as they find their own calling.

Streamlined Systems.

Data + contacts Attendance Communication

Multi-site ministry has an incredible gift of exposing any weaknesses organizationally. Prior to launching our fourth campus, our leaders realized that we had several silos forming throughout our ministry, areas of ministry that were disconnected from the overall vision as they, often unintentionally, pursued their own. Many of our staff and leaders focused primarily on their own needs and ministries. Therefore, it became clear we needed to have an extended staff meeting to discuss the growing divides within our organization. Like a good ol' family therapy venting session, it became apparent that our leadership system had many communication breakdowns. We needed to pause on our desire to launch that new site until we streamlined our system.

One of the tools developed during that time was a series of questions we asked each staff member. We called it, "Who do I go to?"

We asked each of our staff to tell us who they would go talk to for answers to twenty different questions that were relevant to all of our ministries. Here are some sample questions:

- Who should I talk to if I want to start mission work overseas?

- Which ministry could help me start an after school program?

- We have a volunteer who wants to help with lighting at one of our sites, who should I talk to?

- Who should my friend in crisis call?

- Where can I find out more about women's ministry?

- If my friends and I want to start a community basketball league, where should we start?

You get the point.

After our staff answered those questions, it became clear that we were in organizational chaos. Our answers were all over the board. If our staff could not even get the same answers, how could our congregation find the answers? It was discouraging, to put it mildly, but this realization became a tremendous gift to us as it exposed a major problem that needed addressing before starting a new site. Over the next twelve months, we restructured our entire ministry to be more streamlined and ready for our next launch. Stay tuned for more details to come.

Culture of Healthy Feedback.

As previously stated, launching new sites expose the unhealthy parts of an overall ministry. If the leaders in your church aren't strong communicators with one site, having multiple sites will certainly exacerbate the problem. If turf scuffles are present with one site, they will be escalated to full out turf wars with additional sites. While it is nearly impossible to iron out all of the wrinkles in an organization, it is paramount to address obvious issues prior to launch.

Far too frequently, Christians have a sense that giving critical feedback is not loving – when in actuality, the opposite is true. Well-thought-out and meaningful feedback shared in love has the opportunity to grow both individuals and organizations. I know

in church circles, it has become a cliche to
say "iron sharpens iron,"[12] but it is true.
Not only is it true, but it is a biblical concept
that, again, we like to refer to, but don't often
pursue in our communication practices.
Conversely, withholding true thoughts and
opinions keeps the rest of the team in the
dark, holding the overall ministry back
and stunting personal and organizational
growth – or worse – leads to toxic gossip and
misunderstandings. While it is so romantic
to read "the love chapter" of 1 Corinthians 13
at weddings, well-intentioned people seem to
miss the idea that Paul tells us that love also
speaks the truth. Sometimes the most loving
thing people can do for others is to help them
see where they are hurting themselves or
others or to help them see opportunities to
grow, learn and evolve.

We have an agreement with our leadership
teams to obey the *Ten Percent Rule.* This
rule states that it is imperative to share the
unspoken ten percent of thoughts that we
are prone to hold back because, if expressed,

---

[12] Proverbs 27:17

these thoughts or ideas may cause tension or pain within the team. Unfortunately, though, often the person is likely to share it later with a spouse or other close confidant. That not only hurts the team as they miss addressing a deeper issue, but it can damage reputations, create unnecessary gossip organizationally, and foster resentment. To counteract this, we frequently ask if there are any "ten percent" thoughts hanging around the room after we have landed on a decision. Most of the time that leads to circling back for more discussion or addressing felt tension. Overall, it is much healthier for your teams to address the tension while it is simply a sprout of a problem before it takes root and grows into a serious problem. The Hebrew writer counsels us well, *"Pursue Peace with everyone, and the holiness without which no one will see the Lord. See to it that no one fails to obtain the grace of God; that no root of bitterness springs up and causes trouble and through it many be wounded."*[13] A fully grown bitter root among church leaders can sabotage the ability for various campuses to fully function as one.

---

[13] Hebrews 12:14-15

Another way to illustrate it is this: when someone hears something that creates tension within the church or staff, each person has to make a choice to either pour water on the problem or pour gasoline on the problem. In other words, you can bring calm to the tension by asking questions and channeling the problem to the right people in order to find a solution, addressing the issue in a healthy manner, or you can join in with the explosive response by fueling the fire with gasoline gossip, the rolling of eyes, and participating in a "venting" session. It is a simple but effective illustration, and far too many times we chose the latter. Our goal as a church is to create a safe space for people to share their opposing views freely for the good of our church family. Without feedback and healthy communication patterns and structures, the ministry is filled with blind spots and hidden agendas, which only get exposed in a greater manner as the church expands.

Non-Competing Organizational Priorities

Launching a new worshiping community is a life-defining moment as a congregation.

[handwritten margin note: Are we so concerned w/ past wounds + hurt that we're preventing healthy conflict + Honesty?]

It deserves an "all hands on deck" status organizationally. When SpaceX launches a rocket into space, all systems need to declare "go" for the launch to occur. Without a full focus from all of mission control, the results can be devastating.

We learned this lesson the hard way. In 2018, we had a 2.5 million dollar financial campaign to fund our global mission partners along with a few capital projects. During that campaign, we decided to gather a potential launch team for a new campus. That was unwise. The competition for attention was tangibly felt. Consequently, we had a much smaller launch team than expected. In most churches, figuring out the most efficient way to communicate is often an issue. Precious pulpit time is sought after for announcements, knowing that people often perk up and listen to the lead pastor more than any website or mailer.

In evaluation and reflection, if we had the opportunity to walk through that season again, we would have waited until after the fall stewardship campaign to announce the new campus launch team opportunity.

Communication Focus

Our pulpit time was spent investing in campaign time while communicating about the opportunity to be a part of the launch team took a back seat. By pushing the timeline back, we would have had much less competition for advertisement time. Additionally, time spent discussing the most optimal ways to communicate about the campaign was sometimes lacking as we shifted our gaze back and forth between two competing, albeit equally as valuable, initiatives.

As with all of these dashboard points – evidence of God's timing, theological and missional alignment, clearly articulated vision, effective disciple-making pipeline, lay empowerment being the norm, streamlined systems, a culture of healthy feedback and non-competing organizational priorities – discussing these with your leadership teams, staff parishes, and church boards is essential for a healthy launch, and quite frankly, a healthy church. I challenge you to take some significant time to consider the current state of your ministry prior to reproducing in another location.

CHAPTER FOUR
Do You Really Want to Multi-site?

Now that you understand the *whys* and *whats* of the complexity of a multi-site ministry, let me ask the question: do you really want to do this? Functioning as one church in various locations is a significant paradigm shift of "church" as we know it. It is not simply "adding on" to an existing ministry, it is fundamentally changing the mindset of how to do and be the church.

One church in many locations is an easily repeated mantra; it is much more complicated to live out. As campuses have unique needs, the question of how to replicate a similar culture throughout the sites becomes primary. However, the real goal is to hold both the importance of contextualization with the replication of the core mission, vision, and values. It begins with agreeing as a leadership team on your church's DNA or the campus constants. Campus constants are those values or practices that each campus agrees are essential to reproduce.

Campus Constant Examples:

- Mission, Vision, and Values

- Preaching and Teaching

- Worship Arts

- Financial Model

- Governance Model

- Branding and Marketing

- Curriculum

Establishing a multi-site culture takes intentionality and persistence; therefore, it is wise to establish clear and repeatable communication that occurs on many fronts throughout the ministry. Don't miss the intensity of this challenge. Not only will you be shifting the mindset of leaders and congregants, but ultimately, leading a charge to see church in a whole new light. Consider doing the following as you truly evolve into a multi-site ministry:

Preach it.

Preach the value of multi-site. You need to become a multi-site church, not a church with multiple sites. There is a difference. This would seem at first glance to be an obvious point, but for some, it is not common sense. When preaching, find ways to share stories and insights discovered from the other campuses. It can be as simple as saying, "Trevor, our campus pastor at our South Creek Campus was reflecting on this point, and he said…" Or when sharing a testimony, have equal representation from all of the campuses. As the paradigm shifts for the lead pastor, it is astounding how easily it is to forget the importance of celebrating and mentioning what is going on in the life of their other campuses. When this happens, DNA is not transferred and the sites become untethered.

Teach it.

Your church likely has many teaching platforms throughout the week. From adult education classes for new people to membership classes for seasoned believers, and Bible studies to healing ministries, find ways to explain what it means for one church to minister in different locations and how to support one another in that endeavor. Tell your church's story. What compelled you to enter into a multi-site model? When people understand the "why" behind your launch, they are much more likely to engage.

Post it.

This is only true if content is shared to public/non-follower networks

Social Media has clearly become the front door of the church. Be rest assured that the vast majority of people who have walked through your doors in recent years checked you out online first. Celebrate your sites virtually. When something exciting happens at a campus, post it on as many social media platforms as possible. It is wise to post sermons and worship services from each campus. Spread the attention around. Look for people in your congregation who are very active on social media, ask them to consider tweeting message points and state which campus they are attending at the time. Your church's identity will form as one church in many locations as you utilize the many methods suggested here. Social media is an easy grab. It can be done anywhere and at any time. Take advantage of the ease of use,

SEO/SEM + website are front door

we need to get really clear about who is seeing what,

Social media Team

Slack channel

44

flexibility of time, and spread of its outreach.

Listen For it.

People repeat what is reinforced. If what is happening in and around your multiple sites is not being mentioned around the sending church, then it is likely that it has not become your identity. Press on. We typically find that by the time the leaders are tired of talking about a concept, the average Joe in the pews is just starting to understand where the church is headed. Are people talking about your other sites? If not, why not? It is worth asking your leadership teams, church board or pastoral staff.

Confront it.

Do you know what the worst four-letter word is in a multi-site ministry? "Main." Stop using that word immediately. When people use the word main, they are elevating one campus over another. When the words "us" or "them" are used, similar divisions occur. Train your leadership teams to confront words that divide the campuses. Instead, try using the language "sending" church to refer to the initially established campus, or better yet, just refer to each campus by name.

Give Toward it.

Never miss an opportunity to highlight ministry moments during an offering. It is helpful when the campus pastors and leaders meet to share testimonies and celebratory stories. These become invaluable as you pray over the offering during worship. Statements such as, "Did you know that your giving helped to care for a crisis occurring in the community of our (name the campus)?" Year-end giving is another opportunity to create culture as initiatives are highlighted from each campus. As everyone gives to one financial pot, it is inspirational for people to know that their giving goes far beyond their zip code.

Repeat it.

This point is added to re-emphasize the importance of repetitive behavior. Oneness needs to be cultivated consistently, day after day, meeting after meeting and conversation after conversation. As each leader celebrates the multi-site ministry in these variety of ways a new culture will form and the sites will each feel vital within the mission of their church.

Share Stories + Wins
Slack Channel

CHAPTER FIVE
Contextualizing Each Campus

With all of the talk of reproducing the ministry in different locations, as a leader, you may be wondering if joining the new campus will hinder your ability to have a unique ministry impact. One of the criticisms of the modern multi-site movement is that it takes away the site's autonomy and overall decision-making ability. Meaning, an individual campus becomes too manufactured. Thomas White and John Yeats argue in their book, "Franchising McChurch," that it creates "mini-denominations," which negate local church autonomy.[14] This is where a broader view of the movement speaks with wisdom. As the

---

[14] White, Thomas, and John M. Yeats. *Franchising McChurch: Feeding Our Obsession with Easy Christianity.* Colorado Springs: Cook, 2009. pg 189-90.

multi-site model of ministry grew rapidly in the early 2000s, the video venue took center stage as rapidly growing churches, often personality-driven, reproduced the same look and feel in various contexts. That, however, led to some disconnect as each community brought with it unique ministry needs that were not being met. With a one-size-fits-all approach, churches and their multi-sites became bland and predictable and, sometimes, culturally irrelevant.

Contextualization became the in-vogue concept in response to this. The multi-site governance structure evolved. Campus pastors were empowered to make course corrections as they led. Campuses were given more leniency to contextually adapt to the targeted community's needs. Live preaching became more frequent. In short, multi-site matured. Those changes lead to this realization: multi-site is a long-term church planting strategy. Therefore, it is essential for each campus to find its uniqueness as it functions within the multi-site model for years, decades, or even generations depending on its viability.

Ministry is dynamic. For a church to believe the sites will always be in exact lock-step with the others is to misunderstand the life cycle of a church. Parents whose children are still living at home at age 30 have been given the title "failure to launch" for a reason. Parents expect their children to leave home when they are mature and ready. In the complexity of ministry within a rapidly changing culture, it is absurd for a church to believe the multi-site is the end game model for reaching people. Today, we see churches such as The Village Church, under Matt Chandler's leadership, courageously stating that their campuses are moving toward autonomy in order to better reach their communities for Christ. The tension is that as sites contextualize, they need to remain faithful to the existing DNA. Both need to occur simultaneously.

If you are still reading, it is clear that you haven't panicked in counting the cost of entering into the multi-site expedition. Therefore, we can now turn our attention to the details: finding the right campus pastor, training the launch team and developing the overall leadership within the congregation for the expanse of ministry to come.

CHAPTER SIX
Finding the Right Campus Pastor

Leadership matters. While there is always an emphasis on collaboration and empowerment of the laity throughout this book, the role of the campus pastor remains integral to the success of the new site. Because the multi-site model is about many locations remaining as one larger church family, it is important to know and understand what to look for when searching for a campus pastor. When deciphering the calling of a person becoming either a lead pastor of another ministry or the campus pastor in your ministry, there are four different situations to consider depending on the newly called pastor's gift set and preference.

1) Pastoring an existing congregation.

A large contingency of pastors are gifted

and called to shepherd a solid and healthy congregation. They do not want to develop systems and teams from scratch. They want to help keep the ministry moving in the direction it was originally headed. Whether it be folding into the appointment system or candidating in the call system, depending on their denomination's governance model, their next step is to pursue the needs and available options God is revealing to them.

2) *Revitalizing a dying church.*

Some people have the calling, personality type and courage to face the many challenges that come with revitalizing a dying or plateaued church. They naturally understand systems and enjoy challenging the status quo. It may be tempting to place this person in a campus pastor position, but more often than not, this person will fit better being the lead pastor in a revitalization role under their denominational umbrella rather than fit in as a campus pastor of an adoption that will become a multi-site. To revitalize a dying church, this pastor needs innovative ideas and initiative rather than submission to authority and collaboration.

3) *Initiating an autonomous church plant.*

It is relatively simple to discern if someone has a calling to plant a church on their own. They have a strong personal vision and an independent spirit. And, frankly, they usually say it aloud in conversations; they are just that excited! If they are meeting with you, it is typically because they are seeking affirmation and support – financial, mentoring, prayer or as a partner ministry and the like.

4) *Becoming a multi-site campus pastor.*

This person is committed to the vision of the sending church, and they desire to see the established ministry thrive. Their desire is not to be the lead pastor of the overall organization, but they love the idea of reproducing what the church is doing in a new location. S/he has a humble spirit and has no struggle in submitting to the greater ministry teams. Incidentally, it is ideal when the congregation raises their own campus pastor from within the local congregation. It stands to reason that when a church hires a pastor from outside their organization that the new hire is more prone to take the campus in another direction and, thus, precipitate the campus's separation. Discernment is most needed in this situation to be certain that the campus pastor is committed to the vision of the sending church and can submit to other leaders within the church.

All four types of leaders are valuable in their own right, but connecting the local church's need with the right pastoral style is a crucial moment as a church or multi-site is launched. A pastor who is suitable for a church plant or even for the revitalization of a dying congregation looks very different from a pastor in a multi-site ministry context. Nothing would be worse for the campus pastor, new campus, or sending campus to have a pastor gifted as an autonomous planter to take the role of a campus pastor in a multi-site context or vice versa.

Ideally, the best-case scenario is to train up a campus pastor from within the existing staff. This preserves the church constants and vision while maintaining established expectations and work habits that are a part of church culture. However, if the pastor comes from the outside, it is wise to take it slow. A common practice in this case is to hire the outside candidate well before the launch of the campus to ensure enough time and space to learn church culture and build relationships with current team members.

CHAPTER SEVEN

The Core Traits of
a Campus Pastor

When you are ready to train a potential campus pastor from within your church, what are the primary traits you should look for? Although these seem like no-brainers as you train up any staff, this clean and concise model is a healthy place to start when entering into a conversation with a potential campus pastor. These 5 Cs get at the core of a pastor's strengths and weaknesses as you discuss the importance of each one.

- Christ-likeness

- Calling

- Chemistry with others

- Competency in communication

- Courage to obey the voice of God.

The 5 Cs are critical for anyone in ministry. With that established, the following are traits that are specific for multi-site pastors:

They believe in the vision of your church.

Sites flourish when everyone is channeling their energy in the same direction. An organizational stability develops when there is confidence that the leaders of the campuses support the vision and, thus, the overall ministry. One of the fastest ways to deteriorate a relationship between campuses is to have varied visions, but when they are in alignment, a synergy occurs that makes ministry flourish as the leaders support and encourage one another.

It is usually pretty obvious when the campus pastor agrees with the direction of the church – their questions focus on the implementation of the vision instead of pushing back against it. Additionally, passion for or against the vision coming from the core leaders at that particular campus is a good indication of how committed the campus pastor is toward the shared vision. When the site pastor has a love for the overall vision, s/he spreads enthusiasm and encourages support, involvement and commitment throughout the entire church body.

They understand the flow of your church system.

The role of the campus pastor is not to be the centerpiece of the new site. This is where many multi-site ministries break down. Because they are often the "face with the place," most people default to going to the campus pastor with all of their questions. The campus pastor should be the conduit to connect the ministry system together; s/he is not to be the matriarch or patriarch who has the final say on what happens or doesn't happen throughout the campus.

In light of that, let's talk structure. Many ministries are set up like a pyramid. This top down approach to ministry does work well for clarity of authority. The lead pastor or board (or matriarch/patriarch) at the top makes the decisions; the rest of the people within the ministry follow accordingly. This structure works well in a church with a single location and a homogeneous population, but when the ministry spreads out geographically, socio-economically, generationally or the like, ministry contextualization is often lacking. For example, ministry in an urban area will look far different from a rural setting. A top-down pyramid structure often fails to understand the variety and complexity of ministry needs that arise from an expanded ministry. Therefore, a matrix leadership model is often better suited to meet the variety of community needs while maintaining the shared vision.

A matrix governance model is a network that spreads leadership throughout the ministry. Picture a net – when one part of the net is pulled, the other parts are stretched to accommodate. The team works together collaboratively to accomplish the mission. This structure allows for each campus to raise up leaders who remain connected to the rest of the church. In this model, the church has a Lead Team which is comprised of pastoral or director level positions who set the vision and develop material for the campuses. The campus teams work on relationship building and the implementation of the vision of the ministry. With this in mind, the campus pastor then becomes the conduit connecting the person to the various ministry leaders throughout the organization. For example, if a lay leader has a question or feedback regarding a middle school ministry procedure, the campus pastor should refer the leader to the director of middle school ministry from the Lead Team, thus being a conduit of connection, not a top down leader.

They understand the nuanced roles of being a campus pastor.

While the campus pastor will inevitably carry a variety of responsibilities within the structure of the campus, it is helpful to clarify his/her role depending on the multi-site model.

- **The Teacher.** This role is most evident in campuses that have live teaching. As the primary teacher at the new site, it is expected that s/he will find ways to illustrate how their local church is interconnected as one. Comments such as, "I heard a gentleman from our other campus describe how our children's ministry got his daughter excited to come to church like never before" help to interconnect the campuses in subtle yet profound ways. Another way is to remember plural pronouns. Instead of always leading with "I," remembering to add, "When we were preparing this message" or "As we discerned our next steps" will promote unity with the idea that we are one church meeting under different roofs.

- **The Shepherd/Host.** This role is primarily for the campus pastor in a video venue ministry. As with the teacher, it is imperative that they find ways to celebrate the church connections during the announcements and hosting. Additionally, as they build relationships with the congregation throughout the week, they must remember that they are not the end point in a conversation, but the conduit to connect the campus teams to the church wide ministry. This role allows for deeper personal connections to meet individual's needs and to help support and direct them while they grow and serve.

- **The Supervisor/Director.** This role allows for a person who does not have the gift of public communication to have the opportunity to be a campus pastor. S/he is given the positional authority as campus pastor but is often behind the scenes connecting with the host and the leads of each of the ministries for communication purposes between campuses. This role highlights the giftedness of administration and delegation, giving stability to the campus.

To reiterate, campus pastors will need to have a situational awareness to know what type of role needs to be filled in any given moment, however, knowing their primary "lane" of responsibility allows them the best opportunity for success. And regardless of what their core role is, they must remember that they are always the conduit connecting the campus to the greater local church ministry.

They effectively equip others to lead.

Building from the previous point's metaphor of being a conduit in systems connection organizationally, the same can be said of equipping others to lead. It is the job of the campus pastor to train and empower the people within and among the campuses, not to get them all connected to him/herself and definitely not to do all the jobs alone. I cannot stress this idea enough. Plateaus occur when the ministry revolves around a personality or when someone fails to delegate. Therefore, while the personality of the pastor can be a great starting and connecting point, campus pastors must be capable of getting people to look beyond a singular leader and to look instead to the greater ministry of Jesus within the campus.

In their book, *Exponential,* Dave and Jon Ferguson explain a simple yet effective mentoring process:

- I do. You watch. We talk.

- I do. You help. We talk.

- You do. I help. We talk.

- You do. I watch. We talk.

- You do. Somebody else watches.[15]

As the campus pastor mentors his/her core group who also mentors their own core group, teams are developed and connected into the ministry overall. As I have been training my

---

15 Ferguson, Dave, and Jon Ferguson. Exponential: *How You and Your Friends Can Start a Missional Church Movement.* Grand Rapids: Zondervan, 2010.

campus pastors and leaders in this model for several years now, I have discovered one major sticking point. I have started referring to step three as the trap because when responsibility is given to someone in the "you do, I help" phase, a codependent relationship can develop. And sometimes leaders get stuck; the mentor loves being needed, and the mentee loves to be continually guided. In other circumstances, it is hard for the leader to relinquish control when the mentee finds new or innovative ways to "do" or the mentee shows less competence when completing tasks. Yes, this can get much more complicated than the simple phrases express. Unless intentionally addressed, both mentors and mentees may not develop beyond that step, sabotaging the opportunities for other leaders to rise up and join in ministry. Thus, a plateau develops. But don't despair – this coaching should all be occurring in a church culture of healthy feedback, honoring the ten percent rule and leading out of loving relationships. Remember that both parties have the same shared vision!

Wise leaders notice when reproduction stops; the same leaders with the power unintentionally (or sometimes intentionally) block others from getting involved in the ministry. Part of effectively equipping leaders is providing accountability for those involved. It is the campus pastor's job to identify this trap and to keep the campus from getting stuck with the same people doing the same jobs for years. When the campus pastor effectively equips others who equip others, a dynamic campus is established.

They have a deep love for the community in which they will serve.

Does the campus pastor in consideration have a desire to live in and invest in the community where a site could be developed? Dan Reiland, Executive Pastor at 12Stone Church in Georgia, said the campus pastor "must be a fast thinker but a slow walker." In other words, we want campus pastors to have great leadership agility while taking their time to build relationships. They need to grow roots within the community and to study the culture around them. That takes time. For example, they should pick up groceries at the local supermarket, coach their children's little league teams, and talk to their neighbors.

And that is just the start. They must be able to solve problems and diffuse misunderstandings in a way that speaks the local language. I would choose a less gifted campus pastor every time who deeply loves the community over one who has high skill with a lack of love and commitment to the location.

During the first multi-site I had the privilege to be a part of; I studied the demographics of the West Michigan area and discovered a pocket of tremendous opportunity for growth 20 miles to the west of our location. Because of that, I asked our newly selected campus pastor, Alex, to canvas the area. It seemed natural, as he was bi-vocational at the time and worked in that area. As he and his wife drove and prayed through that region, they did not feel prompted to establish a campus there. That caused great tension for me. Alex had all of the criteria we were looking for in a campus pastor, but he and his wife did not have a deep love for that region. However, they did for the center of Grand Rapids, which was 15 miles north of our location. They described various neighborhoods and school systems that quickened their hearts. While that was not our church's initial vision, we discerned that having a campus pastor with a calling and love for the community was worth the change of geographical location. As with any start up ministry, multi-site being no different, love needs to be at the center. Constantly reminding ourselves that without a deep commitment to people and community, ministry can become stale and rote. This is rarely the case when a pastor, campus or not, feels deeply connected to the landscape and its people.

CHAPTER EIGHT
Building the Launch Team

While it is clear that God is the one who makes a church grow,[16] I have found the best way for a pastor to create an atmosphere for growth is through the training and equipping of others for the work of ministry. One of the more fruitful venues for this is through the building of a launch team.

A launch team is a group of people from within the congregation who come together for training to build a base congregation for the new campus. Creating a critical mass that is proportionate to both the sending congregation and the new facility needs to be taken into consideration. Ideally, there would be no fewer than 20 people but could be up to even 100 or more. For every lay person on the launch team,

---

[16] 1 Corinthians 3:6.

the expectation is that each one would bring along two or three additional people to attend the new campus. This takes intentionality. When a team is gathered, trained and sent (for multi-site or any other ministry endeavor), the success is undeniable. And personally, I have witnessed the energy and momentum created by a focused team as being second to none. Consider the following six steps for your upcoming launch:

1. Inspire the Laity. If launching a new campus is like a rocket, then the laity is the jet fuel that powers the engine. This may be starting to sound repetitive, but I cannot emphasize enough the impact of empowered laity. Without a network of deeply committed people to the mission of the launch, it will struggle to find the traction necessary for long-term success. Therefore, inspire the laity within the church to the cause! The new site will likely minister to countless people in extraordinary ways for generations of people in the name of Jesus Christ.

In conversation with launch team members after the new site is planted, they often describe the experience as life defining and worth all of the effort expended. Most people want to be a part of something larger than themselves in life, and this is a worthy calling. Celebrate it. Brag about it. Don't hold back. Inspire the laity. Enthusiasm is an underrated quality. I am not talking about bravado or empty positivity, but genuine care, passion, and enthusiasm for a cause. What better cause than the building of God's kingdom here on Earth? What better cause than seeing broken and downtrodden people come to life through Jesus' healing and love? What better cause then to remind people that they are loved and valued by the God who created the universe? We have much to be excited about. Let's celebrate the joy of the Lord and see how the contagious enthusiasm spreads!

I challenge you to find a revival in Christendom that does not have laity at the core. Every major revival throughout the centuries has been a grassroots movement of men and women who simply loved and worshiped the Lord and wanted to share God's grace with the world. Unfortunately, clergy have not always understood the significant value of a lay person's calling, so there is far too often a divide between the clergy and laity's callings. The Wesleyan Revival of the 1700's was established because John Wesley clearly inspired the laity:

> *Give me one hundred preachers who fear nothing but sin, and desire nothing but God, and I care not a straw whether they be clergy or laymen, such alone will shake the gates of hell and set up the kingdom of heaven upon the earth.*[17]

If you desire to build a strong launch team for your new site, then inspire the laity. Preach about their significance. Lead Bible studies on the Ephesians 4's challenge for the leaders to equip the church for the work of the ministry. Share testimonies of people who have stepped out of the crowd and into their calling. The laity are the key to a successful multi-site ministry within the church. Inspire them.

2. Set High Expectations. People want to be challenged. Start with that premise as you gather a team. As you develop the training, do not "dumb the material down" so they can understand it or so that it feels like a half

---

[17] *The Letters of the Rev. John Wesley, A.M:* 6. London: Epworth, 1931. Pg 272.

commitment that they can easily slip into an already busy schedule. Expect that they will do their due diligence to prepare for the launch. This accomplishes a couple of things. One, it increases the value of the training. If you honor and respect the process, they will likely do the same. Two, it reminds them of the seriousness of the calling to develop a new site as a church. This is a very big deal. The stakes are high. Set the bar high.

It is advisable to have multiple informational meetings as you recruit for the team. The following is a list of expectations to talk through during the meeting:

- I will stay engaged through the duration of the launch season.

- I will pray for and connect with the community.

- I will invest in relationships and invite people to join our ministry.

- I will submit to our church leadership and vision.

- I will volunteer and lead where needed.

You may be wondering if a high standard discourages people from joining the launch team. The answer is *yes*. But do not be concerned! That is actually a good thing; it is exactly what we want. In the multi-site world, always expect that people commit to the cause at different levels. When Brad Kalajainen planted Cornerstone – the church I now serve – he discovered that, in terms of commitment, some people sign in pencil, some sign in ink and some sign in blood. Those who sign in blood are with you through thick and thin. It is sometimes difficult to know who is really "all in" until the end. Having them sign a commitment up front helps to discern those who are just joining the launch team for some distraction or time-filler or mild interest and those who are deeply called to the launch.

The benefit of setting the bar high in the beginning is important because then the launch team actually has little to no attrition. Just the opposite happens – it actually grows and builds momentum toward the launch. However, if the bar is set too low and anyone who simply shows up is on the launch team, it shrinks, leaving the team heading toward the launch day with waning momentum. This is why John Wesley's idea of finding 100 people on fire for the Lord to shake the gates of hell has proven accurate through the years. A small core group with high expectations placed upon them will always outperform a large group of semi-invested people.

3. Clearly Communicate the Timeline.

People follow people who know where they are going. Establish a clear plan with metrics and goals and then advertise...advertise...advertise. Shout it from the rooftops. High capacity leaders guard their time more than their money. While funding is vital to the success of the launch, getting strong leaders is an even greater need. Strong leaders are often pulled in many directions and need to get dates on their calendars sooner than later so that they can stay focused and committed. This big picture planning is also attractive because it keeps the timeline at the forefront. There are no surprises for the high expectations of time commitments, and providing this timeline communicates purposeful strategy. Clearly communicate the timeline. It will draw strong leaders to the team.

At the informational meetings, while recruiting for the launch team, present the launch team syllabus that follows. Include this additional big picture timeline:

- Phase 1 Recruitment – fall: build the team

- Phase 2 Training – winter/spring: 12 weeks, see syllabus for schedule

- Phase 3 Marketing – summer: mission blitz, prayer walking, preview services

- Phase 4 Launch – fall: celebration, follow through, assessment

In addition, hand out a list of benchmarks. The following is an example. Note the Lead and "Timothy" (those being trained up in that area) columns. It is essential that those are each filled in as the launch team is being formed. The key is to have as much ownership by the stakeholders involved within the various lanes of the launch.

	Task	Lead	"Timothy"	Start Date	Target Date
1	Campus Pastor (CP) chosen				09/31
2	Region chosen				10/30
3	CP and location announced to leaders				10/30

4	CP and location announced to church				10/30
5	Launch Team (LT) Recruitment				12/30
6	LT Training Plan established				12/30
7	CP begins licensing				12/30
8	Compile list of potential launch team members				12/30
9	LT personal prayer team established				12/30
10	Establish Campus Budget				12/30
11	LT confirmed				01/01
12	LT Academy begins				01/07
13	Continued mission insight study				03/01
14	Identify area opposition				03/0
15	Building Renovation plan established				04/01
16	Leaders selected from Launch Team				05/13
17	"Just for us" events (BBQ, celebrations)				05/01

Documents like these draw in great leaders, especially when they see the blank spaces, showing room for them to get involved. The whole team needs to feel both the energy and the weight of the launch. Providing these spaces, provides opportunities for ownership.

4. Train them as church planters. Years ago, the traditional model of church planting was known as "The Parachute Drop." A church planter was given some demographic research of growing areas in the community, and then they did the hard work of training and funding for one to three years. After that, they were dropped into the targeted area and were told to network and start a church. This form of planting has a very low success rate (under ten percent) and high burn out rate. One main reason: loneliness. When a single pastor is isolated from other leaders, away from collaboration and synergy, carrying the whole burden of connecting to each and every individual, welcoming them in, it all becomes too heavy of a weight to bear alone. Training a launch team, on the other hand, is the Church's attempt at counteracting the poor results of the parachute drop. Let me explain.

Of the six points in this part of the book, this may be the most crucial one. By training the team as church planters, the campus pastor spends more time on reproducing him/herself into many other planters instead of attempting to build a network with strangers on the street. The network is multiplied exponentially through many people planting the church instead of just one. This has truly changed the narrative. Instead of one exhausted church planter pushing so hard to get the new church off the ground, only to find success ten percent of the time, now there are dozens of "church planters" working together as a launch team, bearing one another's burden and cheering one another on, all the while finding a 90 percent success rate.

The question before us now is obvious – how do we train the launch team? Below is a list of session topics to help train them as church planters.

- Leading yourself

- Leading others

- Mentoring and Discipleship

- Managing conflict

- Understanding multi-site structure

- The power of prayer

- Pitfalls to avoid in multi-site

- The secret to a successful launch

- Post launch planning

The following is a sample agenda for the meetings:

6:30-6:35: Opening Prayer / Worship song

6:35-6:45: Homework discussion from previous week

6:45-7:00: "What's Their Name?"[18]

6:50-7:25: Teaching

7:25-7:45: Breakout into smaller groups[19]

---

[18] This segment helps them to start thinking like church planters. The exercise is simple – have them answer this question,"What's the name of someone you met around town this week?" By discussing this question each week, momentum builds as they begin hearing others speak of networking, building relationships and inviting people in the community to the launch weekend.

[19] Each of the teachings should end with one or two discussion questions for the groups to answer. This accomplishes two purposes: 1) they get to know one another better as they share. 2) the material gets embedded more deeply as each person is expected to answer. Incidentally, we encourage them to shuffle to different groups each week, so they get to know all of the launch team.

7:45-7:55: Discuss questions/comments that arose during breakout

7:55-8:00: Prayer (in circle facing out)[20]

5. Identify their Unique Calling in Ministry. There are two primary approaches to filling the needed volunteer slots in a church multi-site. The traditional way is when the campus pastor or leader responsible for mobilizing volunteers establishes a list of ministry needs and then starts asking people on the team to fill those slots. This "nominations" approach is a time-tested method proven to work. People like to be "called on." They like definiteness and some even like being told what, how, and when to do something. However, experience tells me that the burn out rate for this is high; it often puts people in places of ministry that are out of line with their giftedness. Their passion and energy is often manufactured and forced, leading to more rapid burn out.

---

[20] This is always powerful as the launch team members are facing someone in the community who is in need at that very moment. Someone from the launch team stands in the middle of the circle and reminds everyone, "We've got each other's back, but we are gathered for those not here yet, so let's keep praying for them."

Their willingness may outpace their skill set, and jobs become just that – jobs. Not a holy disturbance they feel compelled to pursue. Of course, there are always chores around a church that need to get done, but as a new site is launched, we want the most gifted and passionate person aligned with the ministry set before them.

Consider another perspective. Ephesians informs us that Jesus is head of the church. With that knowledge, what if we, as leaders, submit to the Holy Spirit's nomination process? The Holy Spirit is our counselor; therefore, He knows our innermost needs, wants, and motives. What if we let Jesus prompt the hearts of our launch team to serve in areas according to His nudges? I know this may sound overly spiritualized or an excuse for not doing our due diligence, but this is the approach I have taken in ministry for many years now, and I can testify to its success.

In his book, the *Purpose Driven Life,* Rick Warren talks about the SHAPE of someone's life. SHAPE is simply an acronym showing the complexity of a person's calling:

Spiritual Gifts

Heart

Ability

Personality

Experiences

I have found this to be better than a standardized spiritual gifts test because there are no standardized people. We are all uniquely made with unique experiences. Because of that, we have each person fill out a SHAPE form during the launch training. They go through a process of looking at each of those areas of their lives. We give them a list of dozens of examples in each category and ask them to write their core answers on their primary SHAPE homework sheet. Under the personality section, we additionally have them share their DISC assessment[21] results. The campus pastor, or nominations leader, sits with each team member and talks through and prays through the responses as they discern together the

---

[21] DISC is a personality tool to help a person to better understand their tendencies. https://www.123test.com/disc-personality-test/

most suitable area of ministry for them to serve in at the new campus.

Believe it or not, you have time to do this. Be patient. To be honest, when you boil down a Sunday morning worship service, the only two essential teams beyond the campus pastor are the worship team and the children's ministry team. This may sound crass, but ushers, greeters, parking lot attendants, service hosts, and the hospitality team are all a blessing but not essential to a public gathering. Not youth ministry, not adult classes, and not even coffee service! It is incredible when all of those pieces are in place, but I would rather patiently wait for a season to have excellent and passion-filled greeters at doors rather than convince people to take those roles who do not have a burden or calling for that ministry. When we leave positions open, eventually someone hears a prompting from the Spirit, steps up, and not only fills the position, but excels in it.

6. Send them Strategically. There is nothing like the energy of a launch season! The community is connected on many fronts: personal invites are sent, various marketing connections are executed. Preview services work out the kinks. Prayers are prayed. The worship team comes together – usually with some surprise miracle eleventh hour new additions – the adrenaline flows! Most significantly, the Lord is worshiped and celebrated in fresh ways. It is a remarkable experience – especially when it is accomplished with every launch team member engaged in the process.

For this meaningful season to begin, just as with the entire training process, the team members need to be strategically sent. How is this accomplished? Finishing the launch team training purposefully. I am an advocate for making the final night of the training similar to a commencement ceremony. Commencement means "to begin." That is a wonderful message to give on the eve of a launch. All of our work has been preparation for what is about to begin.

Consider giving out some sort of "diploma" with a "mission to begin" attached to it along with the verses found in Matthew 28:16-20. One example is this, "As a graduate of the (fill in the name of your church) Launch Team

Academy, I am committed to a lifestyle of investing and inviting from this day forth." Have them sign and date it. After that, have them come forward and be prayed over and commissioned by the campus pastor and/or lead pastor of the church. It can be a deeply spiritual experience. People will be moved as they experience the calling of the Great Commission.

Throughout the next season (typically the summer months), you can blitz the community with loving acts of kindness and marketing touch-points. This is another opportunity to create a benchmark list of outreach tasks for people to take ownership of before the launch. Here are some examples: introduce yourself to city officials, meet police, firefighters and school leaders, attend Chamber of Commerce meetings, connect with local business owners and find ways to collaborate, have coffee with local pastors, establish a web presence, engage on social media, plan a press release, print invite cards, yard signs, flyers, mailers and door hangers, and prepare grand opening celebrations.

This is also an opportunity to evaluate the

four *Ps* of why people attend church. The first is that some people attend a church service because of the Place – they like the actual building or the location itself. Some people will appreciate old architecture or beautiful and bright stained glass windows. Others will enjoy using community space to connect their daily lives with their church life. In the on-line community, it is important to create pre and post service forums for chats, questions and various engaging interactions. This foresight provides a "place" in the virtual world.

The reality is that space affects people. It is interesting to think about that. Others focus on the Pastor – they attend because they like the pastor or the sermons the pastor preaches. Some people are attracted to personality driven churches whether that personality be humble and subtle or gregarious and outgoing. Some have preferences for a deep dive intellectually into an expository sermon, others prefer the hands-on practical approach of a topical sermon. For still others, it is the Programs attached to people. The church meets the needs of what the person is looking for, from Bible study to healing groups, to children's programming or teen outreach. The People – the person has friends or family that attend the church, so they stay connected to that church. There is a marked difference between a church that is welcoming and one that is warm. It is one thing to simply invite someone into your home, and quite another to intentionally ask them questions and connect with them for the purpose of building relationships. Newcomers don't want to feel like outsiders, and yet they often do. Churches become cliquey and dish out generous invites without turning those invites into relationships. We don't want the launch team to become unintentionally exclusive. As we consider the four Ps, it's important to note that some we cannot control, and others we can. In sharing this with the launch team, it can be eye opening and inspiring when they realize that they can directly influence 50 percent of the reasons why people attend church – people and programs.

That inspiration often carries over to the entire church as the launch team is commissioned publicly. During a weekend worship service, the campus pastor shares testimonies from the training experience while incorporating dreams of the future. S/he implores the congregation to be in prayer for the upcoming launch and to invite the people in which they have built relationships with. This creates a synergy of excitement for the entire church body. Jim Griffith, church planting coach, stresses the importance of these early seasons of the launch. At his boot camps for church planters, he shares the following statistics: If a church body is one to three years old, it takes two members of the church to bring one person to the church. If the church is three to five years, it takes seventeen members to bring one person to church. And if the church is five to ten years old it takes seventy-two people to bring one person to church. Seventy-two! The reason for these increasing numbers is obvious. As a church ages, it often loses its zeal for being invitational. Unfortunately, as people become more intertwined with the church family, they lose sight of the greater community, often to the point where they do not have any non-Christians relationships anymore! The exciting thing about the launch season for the congregation is that the fresh start can carry over to the other campuses, consequently reminding the church family of its missional purpose.

Building the launch team has the potential to be one of the most meaningful seasons of developing your multi-site, promoting both personal and collective spiritual growth. Being purposeful by inspiring the laity, setting the bar high, clearly communicating the timeline, training them as pastors, identifying their unique calling for ministry, and sending them strategically sets the tone for not only a healthy and engaging launch for the site, but an opportunity for the sending church to sharpen its existing structures and missional focus. This launch team momentum becomes a spark to ignite passions within the whole church body.

CHAPTER NINE

FAN Your Ministry into Flame

So Christ himself gave the apostles, the prophets, the evangelists, the pastors and teachers, to equip his people for works of service, so that the body of Christ may be built up until we all reach unity in the faith and in the knowledge of the Son of God and become mature, attaining to the whole measure of the fullness of Christ.

Ephesians 4:11-13

One of the reasons I believe the multi-site model has become a growing movement is because it forces the entire church to engage in tangible ways. When active volunteers join the launch team, it frequently leaves ministry gaps in the sending church's ministry. That can cause a jolt to the system when the once flourishing children's ministry, for example, now has to shut down rooms during weekend services because of a lack of volunteers.

This may sound strange, but that is a good thing. Voids and gaps are opportunities. As referenced earlier, this is when the Holy Spirit starts to "nominate" and nudge people to take on new roles within the church.

Ideally, these ministry gaps are filled proactively versus reactively by the person going to the other campus. During the development of the launch team in the many months leading up to the launch, the goal is for the people being sent to the new location to train up a replacement – to find their "Timothy." As we discussed earlier, a leadership pipeline is imperative for each of the sites to flourish as we equip them for the work of ministry. It is often wise to have the mindset of training your replacement. High capacity leaders should always be doing more of the thinking than the doing. What this means is that essentially, a volunteer always has a training and discipleship mindset. As these leaders train and delegate, they then have the opportunity to pursue the next level of leadership that they may be called into, or in a best case scenario, they train up a replacement before they, themselves, experience burnout or a ministry rut – a lack of vision and energy. The staff and leadership of the church are responsible for creating an atmosphere for the people to get plugged in. We call this "FAN" them into flame.

The Emmaus Road event described in Luke 24 inspired this concept. After the crucifixion and, at that point, rumored resurrection of Jesus, some of the disciples were contemplating the events around Jerusalem as they walked home. A man joined them on the journey, and after he left their presence, it became clear to them that it was the resurrected Christ. When they realized it was him, they asked, "Were not our hearts burning within as he opened the Scriptures to us?"[22] We are all on a journey together, and when Jesus speaks to each of us within the body of Christ, our hearts are fanned into flame with a passion to serve and share the great things God has done. We have come to call this a "holy disturbance." A holy disturbance is the calling that keeps you up at night. It is watching a highlight video from

---

[22] Luke 24:32

a mission trip and not just being temporarily moved by an emotional prompt, but instead needing to participate with urgency. It is seeing the broken and abused and feeling a holy anger or frustration that leads you not to just vent to a friend, but rather think strategically to find ways that God can intervene on the behalf of the oppressed. It is a passionate desire to want to create the most welcoming atmosphere possible as an usher, the first impression a newcomer gets. Every Christ-follower has a spark of passion and purpose, and it is our job to FAN that into flame.

The goal at our local church is to FAN into flame 100 percent of our congregation. We want to see every heart that has a flame of personal calling to be channeled. That kind of burning passion for the Kingdom of God needs to be supported and nurtured by the Church. FAN is an acronym for our staff and leadership to remember their primary purpose in equipping the church for ministry. Our strategy to connect the congregation in ministry at each site is the following:

Face to Face

Ask Questions

Network Them with Others

Building a team of ministers within the church cannot be formulaic. It is efficient to have someone take a Spiritual Gifts Assessment and then just plug them into felt needs. Many take this approach. While it has merit, it discredits the idea that above all, ministry is relational. Disciple making is dynamic and fluid based on each person's uniqueness. That is why the first step is to meet with people face to face.

Face to Face

In an ever more distracted and disconnected society, we believe that just emailing or texting people when they show signs of a developing holy disturbance is a way to douse the spark of ministry passion. Spending time with each other gives value and validates a person's desire to pursue his/her calling. God designed us to spur one another on! Personal relationships are vital to our spiritual health and to the mission of God.

"Do not neglect meeting together..." [23]

"Jesus sent the disciples out two by two..." [24]

"Have equal concern for one another..." [25]

Jesus modeled this when he spent time with his twelve disciples. Because he asked them questions and networked with each of them and the others through the Holy Spirit, they, in turn, did the same. They met face to face with people, and their personal ministries multiplied as they built the church we experience today! Do not underestimate the power of personal connection.

Ask Questions

Did you know that Jesus asked lots of questions? He was inquisitive, and consequently, people asked him questions back. Interestingly, of all the questions he was asked, He only answered three. He most often responded with a question! What does that

---

[23] Hebrews 10:25

[24] Mark 6: 7

[25] 1 Corinthians 12:25

tell us about our Savior? Really...what do you think that tells us?

Questions cause people to internalize the answer, giving them a chance to really own their responses, passions, and plans. Questions are as much for your sake as they are for theirs. As they verbally process their answers, they begin to not only own, but start to both actualize their ministry goals and help to share them with the potential team they may be working with. This takes time! Ask many open-ended questions, try to avoid yes/no answers.

Here are some starter questions:

- Tell about an experience when time went quickly while serving.

- What has kept you from diving deeper in that ministry?

- Describe a time when God really used you.

- What is happening in this world that frustrates you or breaks your heart?

- What is Jesus stirring in your heart?

- What are you going to do about that burden?

- Or if they want to start a ministry, consider some of these:

- Who are some other people with a similar disturbance?

- Would this ministry fit into the vision of this church site?

- What is your leadership style? Which other type of leaders do you need for support? How can we help with the next steps?

- How can I pray with and for you?

Listen carefully as they answer. Take notes so that you can recap their answers. Many times, leaders will "hear" both the advantages of their plan and the opportunities they will have to rework their expectations and strategy.

Network Them with Others

People's ministry will often be outside the walls of the church. It may be in their home, work, school, or other community or parachurch organizations that are already flourishing in that area. That is okay. Let me repeat that – it is okay. Empowering the church to "leave the building" is an opportunity to be the church to surrounding communities. Too many times, people inside the church feel as though they need to execute their holy disturbance within the church walls. We need to reinforce the idea that the church is not a building, and that there are many, many opportunities to serve people well outside the church community. Additionally, as they network with others, they will be better able to name and understand their own leadership style.

CHAPTER TEN
Primary Leadership Styles

The subsequent list of leadership styles has been extremely helpful in establishing any well-rounded team but is especially true in the early days of a new campus. While leaders can have multiple styles based on what is needed in any given situation, no one person can fulfill all eight types. That affirms our need for one another. Yes, this, of course, is becoming a common theme throughout the book. Sorry, folks, there is no way around it. All of these leaders have an important role in building a sustainable ministry.

As you read this list, ask yourself which of these is your natural default. In addition, an even more crucial question is, do your current teams have all eight of these leaders represented?

1) *Big Picture Leader.*

Every team needs a vision of the future – a picture of where they are headed. This is vital for the success of a team. Abraham was able to sustain the heart of his family on their long journey to an unknown land by visualizing the big picture of God's multi-generational call upon them. The big picture leader is not always aware of the "how" of the story, but they possess the "wow" that inspires the followers.

This kind of leader is able to cast the big picture vision for the multi-site and/or ministry that is launching to help sustain the campus. S/he typically has a contagious enthusiasm that is rooted in faith and is not afraid of a challenge, knowing that only God can make this happen. This leader's weakness (or shadow side) is lack of strategic and/or detailed thinking. They often do not know how to accomplish that large vision, and therefore can lose the hearts of the followers as they get deeper into the journey. Without strategy, big visions lose momentum quickly. Hence the reason for the other leaders on these pages.

2) Startup Leader.

The startup leader is often the most extroverted and gregarious person on the team. When they speak, people listen. Their contagious engagement of the big picture gets the crowd to follow. They do not always see with perfect clarity the fullness of the ultimate destination, but they see enough to inspire the people. The Apostle Paul was certainly a startup leader, planting church after church. He would establish leadership within that new congregation and would move on after the launch was off the ground.

This type of leader is resourceful and optimistic even in the gloomiest of seasons. The old saying rings true, "People follow people who know where they are going." Their excitement for the future is so inspiring that people gather to participate. Having said this, the startup leader needs to be aware of their perceived flakiness. After launch, they are prone to get bored and move on to another new ministry that needs some catalytic energy. Like a rocket that uses 70 percent of its fuel on takeoff, this leader will disappoint people if they fizzle out at the new site or ministry as they become distracted and move on to the next mission.

One of challenging lessons learned in my early years of pastoral ministry revolved around this type of leader. Ben began attending our church and came to life as he came alive in his faith. He heard about ministry ideas, saw the vision, gathered the crowd and started the ministry. Season after season, new ministries were developing in the church. However, my frustration grew as very few of them lasted after a year or two. In reflection, I came to realize that Ben was simply a startup leader and that I should not have expected him to fill the other seven leadership roles. I failed to build leadership teams around him for sustainability.

With that example in mind, it is imperative to the health of your launch team not to be mesmerized by the bright light of excitement garnered by the startup leader's energy. As they are gathering a following, surround them with the other types of leaders for the overall health and sustainability of the ministry.

3) Procedural Leader.

Launching is complicated and dynamic with many moving parts. The fog of war is an accurate metaphor. The big picture and startup leaders often cause some chaos in the midst of all of the excitement and energy. Therefore, someone is needed to manage this mess. Enter the procedural leader. This type of person may not have the gift of developing the vision and rallying the crowd, but they are certainly the key to moving forward as they create an order and focused system.

Consider Moses. He was a big picture and startup kind of leader. After rallying the Hebrews in the Exodus from Egypt, he quickly became overwhelmed. His father-in-law became his procedural leader and guided him well.

> *Moses listened to his father-in-law, Jethro, and did everything he said. He chose capable men from all Israel and made them leaders of thepeople, officials over thousands, hundreds, fifties and tens. They servedas judges for the people at all times. The difficult cases they brought toMoses, but the simple ones they decided themselves.*[26]

---

[26] Exodus 18: 24-26

Jethro is as much of a hero in the story as Moses. His methodical approach to leadership created an atmosphere of order and stability, and, thus, proved that procedural leaders are vital to the mission.

One note of caution. The mantra of this type of leader is typically something like "procedure prevents problems." Phrases like these can be perceived by spontaneous and risk-taking leaders as being a wet blanket that douses the passionate fire of the launch. The tension can quickly rise within the team. It is crucial that the team understand the importance of every leadership style to continue fostering respect for each other. When the procedural leader asks specific questions to the startup or big picture leader, they may simply hear "no," and assume that those leading questions are just trying to block the task. Learn to be less defensive. On the other side, if you are a procedural leader, consider using the word "wow" before the word "how." Celebrate the idea, help fan the fire into flame and offer help and insight on how to focus that passion together, strategically. Consider statements such as these: "Wow, I love that idea and the excitement that's building within the team. I'd love to help develop a next steps plan with you." Or "I am really enjoying all of the energy you are developing with the vision, can I help develop a budget to focus on a long term and sustainable strategy?" Note the collaborative nature of the questions. The new site has its greatest opportunity for success when the teams truly support one another.

4) Team Builder.

This type of leader has a sense for bringing people together. They can naturally see the gifts and abilities of each person and can identify potential personality friction and establish healthy connecting points with people. This person has a strong "human resource" tendency and has high situational and emotional awareness – interpersonal intelligence. In other words, they can read the room.

People are inspired by them because they feel appreciated, respected, and understood. This may be stating the obvious, but Jesus had a strong tendency toward leading this way. He took twelve ordinary teenagers with a variety of personality types and turned them into world changers. He saw the deeper uniqueness in Peter, James and John, and elevated His expectations by giving them extra leadership training through their three years together. Those of us who have a team building calling of leadership would be wise to do the same.

5) Bridge Builder.

This leader is essential to the team because they have the emotional intelligence to sense the tension between individuals and/ or groups, and they are good at networking others who may not see the connection themselves. Moreover, they help build the bridge between disagreeable groups in order to make progress toward peace and reconciliation. With this type of leader, it seems as if their blood pressure goes down when the tension rises within the team.

Prophets such as Micah, Isaiah or Jeremiah are excellent examples of bridge builders. They see people enslaved or people in trouble or in sin, and they have no problem calling it out. This leader can see the alternatives that no one else may be able to see. This is essential during the launch season to have a person who can be the resident "counselor" on the team. Launching a new campus inevitably turns up the heat as vision and procedure is often challenged.

6) Critical Crossroads.

Life is dynamic and fluid. Ministry is no different. Every ministry, including the launching of a new campus, goes through a life cycle. Within a life cycle, there are critical crossroad moments. As your body grew, it went through a critical crossroads moment, called puberty in which it changed from being a child to an adult. These moments are essential for growth. Within multi-site, the body of Christ comes to many critical crossroad moments. Should we buy or rent in light of the new developments this year? Do we hire any staff if no one from the launch team fills these significant roles? Do we change our location in light of discovering another church is planting in the same place? During the pandemic, many churches were asking if they should change their launch date. The answers to these vital questions are essential.

Thus, they need a discerning spirit. A critical-crossroads leader analyzes the situation and offers tremendous guidance.

Personally, I cannot make major decisions without this person's insight. They see the ultimate goal over the immediate crisis. They have the God-given ability to see several steps ahead and the potential pitfalls that come with the various options on the table. Esther is a great example of a critical crossroads leader who realigned Israel during "such a time as this"[27] When I share these various leadership roles with the team and then tell a specific person that I see them as a critical-crossroads leader, they often rise to the occasion in even more surprising ways. Every time they pray with more fervency and engage in the ministry in profound ways.

7) Cheer Leader.

This may not appear to be a significant leader within the team, but a cheer leader's influence and importance is invaluable, hence the distinction between cheer leader

---

[27] Esther 4:14

and "cheerleader." This leader is an active participant in the team who doesn't just sit on the sidelines. Multi-site ministry is stressful and can be filled with multiple and various distractions – especially during the launch season. Cheer leaders have the wisdom to say thank you. To send notes of encouragement. To remind us to persevere to the finish line. To notice the hundreds of unnoticed details to create a grateful culture throughout the team.

This leader knows how to celebrate. This leader knows how to publicly recognize others' successes. This leader exudes positivity and understands what it means to have the joy of the Lord. And to be honest, sometimes our churches are filled with the theology of suffering. It's all too easy when doing the endless work of the ministry to get discouraged or to just keep on keeping on without much fun, without celebrating the wins all around us. Jesus feasted. Jesus celebrated. Jesus valued coming together to bolster one another when enthusiasm waned.

Never underestimate the importance of this type of leader on the team. The early church saw this as essential as the apostles renamed, Joseph, one of their teammates in ministry, Barnabas – which literally means encourager.[28] As the launch team faces many challenges and attempts to make all of the right moves, it is imperative to have someone speaking life to the team. Giving thanks in all circumstances is, after all, at that heart of God's will for us in Christ Jesus.[29]

8) Pastoral Leader.

Similar to the cheerleader, the pastoral leader is vital to the health of the team. People need to know that they are loved, cared for and prayed for. This type of leader has a strong gift of discernment, observation and shepherding. They can see when someone is hurting. They are called to invest in the flock and to protect them from the wolves of life. Too many times we assume that once someone has "found" Jesus, they have "found" healing. But healing is a process. Often it takes years of nurturing and encouragement, and sometimes even counseling for an individual to experience the

---

[28] Acts 4:36

[29] 1 Thessalonians 5:18

true fullness of Christ's power of restoration. Leaders are no different. To acknowledge that leaders, as well as congregants, have a need for a pastoral leader is life-giving.

This leader comes alongside the team to assess and promote healthy spiritual growth within the team and beyond. The pastoral leader is often the leader who reminds us that this is not our church, but God's. The calming presence of the pastoral leader puts issues into a Godly perspective so that, in a sense, the team does not get too caught up in either vision or people or procedure, and can be reminded of the sovereignty and power and care that comes with serving the loving Father.

Acts 6 beautifully describes the need for leadership roles in ministry. As the Apostles carried the mantle of teaching, prayer and evangelism throughout the land, they appointed seven others to care for daily distribution of food and care for those in need. These servants and shepherds cared for others in tangible ways. As you meet with your team and network them together through the FAN process, challenge them to step up in their various leadership roles to carry the mantle.

Multi-site flourishes when all people are engaged in the movement and all leaderships roles are acknowledged, understood, and celebrated. But what happens when all of the aforementioned doesn't occur?

CHAPTER ELEVEN
The Common Fails in Launching a Campus

As stated throughout this book, multi-site ministry has a high success rate because of the mutual long-term support it offers between each of the campuses. When one has a rough season, the other sites can add volunteers, finances and spiritual support to help in the triage. As it recovers, it can reciprocate for the inevitable downtimes the other campuses will experience. Therefore, more often than not, multi-site ministries flourish. However, in those few times they do not succeed, patterns have emerged through the years to help us better to understand why.

1. A system breakdown.

One of the most frequent reasons for a failure to launch is that the structure could not sustain it. People were either unclear regarding the chain of command or the channels of communication were jammed. The primary default to counteract these problems is to develop a centralized form of governance. In these cases, the core leadership team is responsible for developing vision and curriculum, the campus leaders are responsible for implementing and distributing the vision and material, so they have the time to build relationships, teams and networks. The key in this structure is to establish a clearly diagramed flow chart that includes each and every leader within the ministry.

A few years ago, our three campuses were struggling to communicate effectively with one another. At the time, we were in the initial stages of the possible adoption of another church for a fourth campus. This became a critical crossroads moment for us as many leaders stated how unprepared we were. Therefore, we elevated one of our core leaders to the position of the director of multi-site. Kevin became known as the glue between the campuses. His sole job was to identify and report glitches between the campuses and any leadership gaps. Within weeks, the tension subsided and dreams of a church adoption were widely embraced.

2. The lead pastor does not embrace the personal changes needed.

If asked, virtually all lead pastors verbalize an excitement to reach other communities and to expand their ministry. But saying and doing are two different worlds. The leadership needed with multiple locations is vastly different from a typical ministry gathering in one geographical location. One of the most drastic shifts needed is the releasing of control. Pastors are typically known for micro-managing or at the very least being in the know on all of the details of the ministry. Multi-site cannot flourish under that kind of paradigm.

Healthy delegation is the key. Craig Groeschel has described it this way on his podcast,[30] "Give someone a task and you gain a follower. Give someone authority and you gain a leader." Pastors get beat up in ministry. That is a given. During my ordination, my

---

[30] https://www.life.church/leadershippodcast.

bishop said to us, "You are becoming more and more like Jesus every day. The people who cheer you on today will want to crucify you tomorrow." Because of this reality, pastors are prone to become micromanagers over time. If they can control the environment, they can possibly minimize the criticism aimed in their direction. When their default is over-controlling a task, their influence and ability to multiply diminishes drastically. That cycle sabotages the multi-site system.

Additionally, it is unfortunately common for a lead pastor to go to one extreme or the other. One is for the pastor to be so energetic about the new site that the other location(s) get jealous of their constant references. The innocent joy can be perceived as favoritism thus causing an unnecessary rift between the sites. The other extreme is to rarely acknowledge their existence. It is quite obvious when the lead pastor does not embrace the other sites. They rarely reference them, and if they do, it is in contrast to the "main" site where they are primarily working. They do not see anything wrong with referring to their site as the main because it birthed the others and is clearly the largest contributor financially. If you are a senior leader and are in agreement with the last couple of sentences, then you may be or will become part of the problem.

3. The campus pastor forgets where s/he came from.

Launches bring such energy and excitement; however, it can be difficult to fend off the pride that frequently follows. Additionally, because the new site feels so vulnerable in the first year or two, the needs often seem so vital for its survival in comparison to the other campuses. While a myopic focus is essential in the early days, if left unchecked it can become an unhealthy and controlling habit that unintentionally leads to a rift between campuses.

As referenced earlier, this type of tension can be identified with the use of "us" versus "them" language or "here" versus "there." For example, hearing comments such as; "We came to this campus because they were not willing to take risks like we are." "I used to attend at that site, but they did not use my gifts like they do here." "I just feel so much energy here. Things were getting stale over there." "I sense an amazing move of the Holy Spirit over here." Comments like these can subtly plant seeds in the mind of the campus pastor. The subversive nature of these comments can twist the thinking of the most loyal site pastors.

Over time, this can lead to an unhealthy form of competition between the campuses. The competition is rarely overt, but it can become an unspoken judgment in the mind of the campus pastor during meetings or in conversations about the larger church as a whole. For clarity's sake, competition is not bad, in fact, it can and often does bring out the best in us. However, if left unchecked, competition between campuses can corrode the health of the ministry. One way to avoid this is to have the campus pastor carry another major responsibility for the church overall. If s/he is responsible for the overall health of the small group ministry, for instance, it can lift them above the myopic focus of the individual campus in order to see the bigger picture.

4. Empowering unhealthy leaders.

Church plants in any form are prone to attract unhealthy people. The reason this frequently occurs is because a new church can be a fresh start for those who have burned bridges in the past for whatever reason. The church planter/campus pastor, who is often feeling the pressure to grow the launch team, can be tempted to fill positions with any warm body that willingly comes along to lend a hand. This pattern must be guarded against at all costs. It is essential for the long term health of the campus that a vetting standard remains intact throughout the launch season and beyond.

How does a church guard against empowering unhealthy leaders? The 5 Cs of Character, Competency, Calling, Chemistry and Courage, described earlier, are filters that can certainly help the leadership teams to select the best candidates for the needed ministry positions. It is crucial to not compromise while building a team. Healthy leaders create healthy systems which naturally develop an attractive church culture for the community. When filling leadership positions, I frequently ask myself, "Will my future self be pleased with my decisions by this time next year?" If the answer is "No," I have found it is far better to suffer the organizational awkwardness of unfilled positions now than to face the destructive problems of an unhealthy leader entrenched within the church later.

Another way to guard against this is to consider what kind of influence the person currently has or should have in the future. That influence translates into power. Generally speaking, there are three types of power that people potentially carry when in a leadership position:

- Positional Power

- Relational Power

- Perceived Power

Positional power is when the person was officially voted on or hired into that position. Within the ministry, the people have agreed that this person is the lead of ministry X. They are in an agreed upon position of power within the church system. Relational power is the person who is not officially the leader, but when they speak, people listen. This person is networked and has clear influence within the church. Their power is felt through their extensive network of connections to others. Perceived power lies within the person. This is often the catalyst for tension within the campus. The person may have served in an influential position in the past, therefore, they now assume they are the leader of that ministry at the new campus. They may have no positional or relational power, but within their mind, when they speak people should listen. Healthy campuses develop when campus leaders understand the power dynamics at play within the new site.

As the campus journeys through the launch process, the needs are plentiful. And as the launch date approaches, the pressure builds and compromises can easily be justified. If unmonitored, unhealthy leaders can get into leadership positions and rapidly create a toxic environment. One church I was coaching years ago fell into this unexpected struggle over the landscaping at their new location. A woman from the launch team volunteered to help plant some flowers and lay some mulch. Since no one else stepped up, she had developed some perceived power in her mind. When other people started adding to the landscaping without asking her, tension rapidly grew. What was supposed to be an exciting three weeks leading up to the launch date, turned into misunderstandings, hurt feelings and destructive gossip throughout the church and worse yet, throughout that small town. All of the marketing efforts were certainly diminished by the internal feud that spread into the streets. And that was just over flowers.

5. An undefined financial structure.

This point may be obvious, since any organization will struggle under mismanaged finances. Within the multi-site world, three primary financial approaches have surfaced, and it is necessary to find which one fits your particular organizational needs.

One Budget: This has become the most prevalent multi-site option as each campus' offering collection is added to the total church budget. Each site then has line items within the overall budget. This breeds success because it is easily documented and displayed in finance reports for full transparency and collaboration.

Separate Budget: In this case, each site has its own budget. It is typically produced and analyzed by one common finance team; however, there are few shared resources. One of the great benefits of multi-site is the instant support, when one is struggling the other sites can carry the load financially. When there are separate budgets, there can be less of a desire to share resources.

70/20/10: In this model, 70 percent of the offering taken at the site goes to that site. 20 percent goes to the multi-site central services which can be everything from administration to curriculum development. The remaining ten percent goes into a fund for future sites. This model has been embraced by many for the value it places on reproduction. It produces more of a sustainable approach to ministry financially.

Each of these financial systems have shown success. The failure comes in the lack of fully embracing a plan and clearly communicating the financial structure throughout the church organization.

6. *The loss of a missional mindset.*

The model I have proposed in this book regarding the training of a launch team has a definite shadow side. The best word to describe it is entitlement. When people have invested in a year of training, networking with the community and owning the weight of the launch with the campus pastor, a spirit of ownership of the campus can quickly follow after the launch. Another way to describe it is people can get territorial about their "new baby campus." If not addressed strategically, the focus can become all about the new site and thus an inward clique can form. But that should not be the end game. The purpose is to connect the community with Christ.

Additionally, burn out can be a real problem for the launch team when the adrenaline rush of the opening weekends burns off and reality of the hard work sets in. This is the primary reason we teach the Tuckman Model of Team Development[31]

---

[31] https://infed.org/mobi/bruce-w-tuckman-forming-storming-norming-and-performing-in-groups/

during the launch training. What this model teaches are the stages teams go through. This was developed in 1965 as four stages: *Forming, Storming, Norming, Performing.* Each of these stages are important in the life of the launch team; however, in 1977 Bruce Tuckman added what I believe to be the most important stage of a team as it pertains to multi-site; the *Adjourning* stage. If the launch team does not adjourn as a team, getting commissioned and sent as a campus, ready to reach the community for Christ, it can quickly slip into an inward focused and territorial clique and thus become another plateaued small church with little impact on the community. Therefore, as stated before, it is helpful to have a final celebration as a launch team post launch to celebrate the victories and to re-establish the new vision for the campus overall with all of the people included.

As the new campus gets a few months beyond the launch, it is beneficial to have a church wide meeting. During that "family meeting," it is great to share testimonies of people you have reached thus far and to re-establish the overall missional vision of why the new campus was launched in the first place. As the vision is laid out, it can be helpful to share very tangible ideas of how to keep connecting with the community. Ideas such as eating at the same restaurants to establish relationships with the staff, remembering the importance of networking with people within the community. It's also important to be reminded that we live in a TGIF world; Twitter, Google, Instagram and Facebook. Having a missional mindset means watching what you post – -everything you post represents our ministry and more importantly, Jesus Christ. Pursue holiness in all things, because we are not set apart from the world, we are set apart for the world. Our witness matters.

Afterword

Multi-site ministry is complex. The danger of writing a book on this subject is that we can quickly believe it is about following a formula versus remembering that the head of the church is Jesus, not the dynamic campus pastor or a perfectly designed church structure. What I have fallen in love with in launching multi-sites is that each situation is unique to the moment in time, thus a reliance on the Holy Spirit's guidance and counsel is imperative. And now, as we face ministry in a post-pandemic world, group gatherings have changed, making a willingness to pivot and adjust the ministry key to our continued witness.

Ephesians tells us that Jesus died for the church and has thus proven to us that he is fully committed to the plan of reaching the world through his bride. We certainly have some messy times in our history as a church, but she is still worthy of a full investment of our time, talents and treasure. As you think about what our world lacks, no government can truly fix the needs of this world. No community action group or massive amount of money can solve the world's problems. Why? Because those things cannot fix the human heart. As the Body of Christ, we have the great privilege of carrying the Good News of the Gospel that truly transforms the human heart. As we continue to find ways to be effective and relevant in a rapidly changing world, our multi-site efforts will continue to bear fruit for generations to come.

What is The Greatest Expedition?

The Greatest Expedition is a congregational journey for churches, charges, or cooperative parishes led by a church Expedition Team of 8-12 brave pioneering leaders. The purpose of The Greatest Expedition is to provide an experience for Expedition Teams to explore their local context in new ways to develop new MAPS (ministry action plans) so you are more relevant and contextual to reach new people in your community. Updated tools and guides are provided for the church's Expedition Team. Yet, it is a "choose your own adventure" type of journey.

The tools and guides will be provided, but it is up to the church's Expedition Team to decide which tools are needed, which tools just need sharpening, which tools can stay in their backpack to use at a later time, what pathways to explore, and what pathways to pass.

the greatest
EXPEDITION

The Greatest Expedition provides a new lens and updated tools to help your Expedition Team explore and think about being the church in different ways. Will your Expedition Team need to clear the overgrown brush from a once known trail, but not recently traveled? Or will the Expedition Team need to cut a brand new trail with their new tools? Or perhaps, will the Team decide they need to move to a completely fresh terrain and begin breaking ground for something brand new in a foreign climate?

Registration is open and Expedition Teams are launching!

greatestexpedition.com

the greatest
EXPEDITION

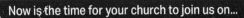

Made in the USA
Columbia, SC
13 June 2021

40022824R00076